BLUE WHALES

BY PATRICIA HUTCHISON

Published by The Child's World®
1980 Lookout Drive • Mankato, MN 56003-1705
800-599-READ • www.childsworld.com

Acknowledgments
The Child's World®: Mary Berendes, Publishing Director
Red Line Editorial: Editorial direction and production
The Design Lab: Design
Amnet: Production

Design Element: Shutterstock Images
Photographs ©: Cordier Sylvain/Hemis/Corbis, cover, 1;
iStockphoto, 4, 20; Holly Fearnbach/Southwest Fisheries
Science Center/NOAA Fisheries Service, 5, 18–19;
Isabel Beasley/Southwest Fisheries Science Center/NOAA
Fisheries Service, 6–7; Visuals Unlimited/Corbis, 10, 22;
Robert Harding Specialist Stock/Corbis, 11; Frank and
Frances Carpenter collection/Library of Congress, 12–13;
Alex Kol/Shutterstock Images, 15; Sophie Webb/Southwest
Fisheries Science Center/NOAA Fisheries Service, 16;
Ruth Peterkin/Shutterstock Images, 21

ISBN 9781631439667
LCCN 2014959637

Printed in the United States of America
Mankato, MN
July, 2015
PA02264

ABOUT THE AUTHOR

A former teacher, Patricia Hutchison enjoys traveling with her family. She's visited the Pacific Ocean along the coast of Big Sur, California. Hutchison enjoys writing books for children about science and nature.

TABLE OF CONTENTS

CHAPTER ONE

GIANT MAMMALS

**Blue whales, such as this young one, are
the largest animals in the world.**

Blue whales are the biggest animals to ever live on Earth.
They are larger than any dinosaurs were. Blue whales grow
more than 100 feet (30.5 m) long. A blue whale can weigh
up to 200 tons (181.4 t). Its heart alone weighs as much as
a small car. Its tongue weighs as much as an elephant.

Like all whales, blue whales are **mammals**. They must come to the ocean's surface to breathe. They each have a blowhole on the top of their heads. It is like a huge **nostril**. It is so big a small child could crawl into it. The whale surfaces and blows air out its blowhole. The spray can shoot 30 feet (9.1 m) in the air. Then the whale breathes in. It takes in enough air to fill a van. Once it has air, the whale can dive and swim underwater.

Spray shoots up from a blue whale's blowhole.

Blue whales are named for their skin color. Underwater, they look blue. Out of water, they are a spotted blue-gray. Their spots are like human fingerprints. No two blue whales have the same pattern of spots. Harmless **diatoms** stick to the whale's belly. They give it a yellow color. Blue whales have broad, flat heads. Their bodies are long and tapered. Wide, triangular flukes on their tails help them move through the water.

The skin of a blue whale has blue-gray spots.

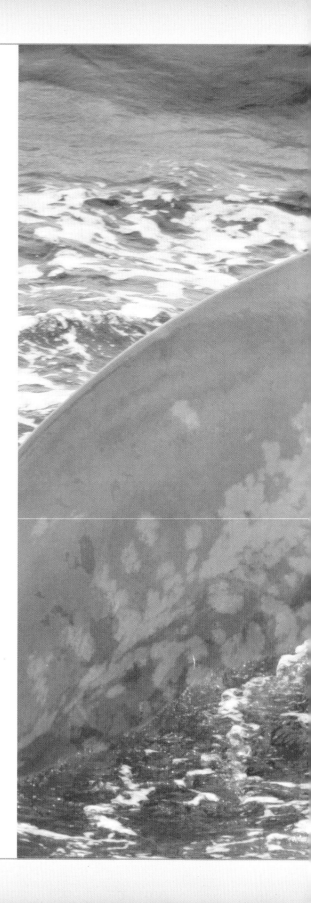

These giants belong to a group called baleen whales. Their mouths have a row of plates. The plates are lined with long, bony fringe called baleen. This fringe helps the whales filter their food from the water. Blue whales eat mostly **krill**. They can eat up to 4 tons (3.6 t) every day. To eat, a blue whale dives approximately 1,600 feet (487.7 m). It opens its huge mouth. It takes in a gulp of water. A pouch on its throat expands. Its tongue pushes the water back out through the baleen plates. The krill are left behind in the whale's mouth. The whale swallows the tiny krill whole.

Blue whales live in the world's oceans.

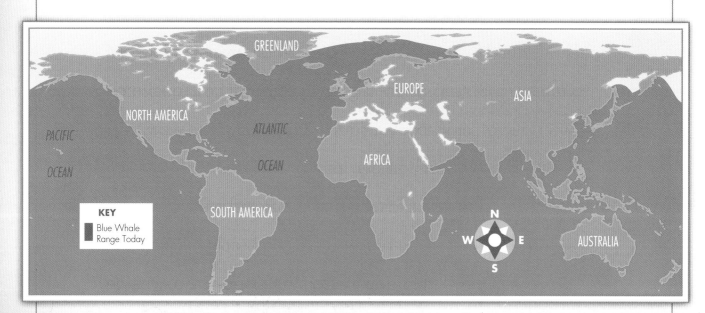

KEY
Blue Whale
Range Today

GREENLAND
EUROPE
ASIA
NORTH AMERICA
ATLANTIC
PACIFIC
OCEAN
OCEAN
AFRICA
SOUTH AMERICA
AUSTRALIA

Blue whales live in all the oceans on Earth. Some spend summers in cold water near the poles. They travel to the **equator** in winter. Others stay in the same area all year. The largest number of blue whales live in the eastern part of the North Pacific Ocean.

Blue whales live longer than many other animals. Scientists count the layers of a dead whale's earwax to learn their age. The oldest known blue whale was 110 years old. But most live 80 to 90 years. The giant whales can start having calves around age ten. Female whales give birth to one calf. These big babies weigh up to 3 tons (2.7 t). They are approximately 25 feet (7.6 m) long. Mothers push their newborn babies to the surface to take their first breaths.

UNDERWATER THUNDER

The blue whale is one of the loudest animals on Earth. It communicates using pulses, moans, and groans. A blue whale's call is louder than the sound of a jet taking off! It can be heard underwater up to 100 miles (160.9 km) away.

Blue whales usually swim alone or in pairs. They sometimes form small groups. Scientists think they form close bonds in these groups.

Blue whales make sounds to help them move through the dark ocean. The sound bounces off objects in the ocean. Then the sound travels back to the whales. It tells the whales where the objects are. Blue whales swim at about 5 miles per hour (8 kmh). But if in danger, they can swim up to 20 miles per hour (32 kmh).

Some blue whales choose to swim in pairs.

CHAPTER TWO

THREATS TO BLUE WHALES

Human activities have put blue whales at risk.

Blue whales are large creatures. They have few natural **predators**. But these animals are **endangered**. There are only 10,000 to 25,000 blue whales in the oceans. People are the largest threat these giant whales face. Human activities have killed many blue whales.

People have hunted whales in the United States since the 17th century. They made oil from whale fat. People used whale oil as a fuel for lamps and to make soap and shoe polish. It was also an ingredient in margarine. Although many whales were hunted for their oil, the blue whale was not. The giant animals were too powerful and fast to catch. But then the **harpoon** cannon was invented. It made it easy for **whalers** to kill blue whales. Whalers killed hundreds of thousands of blue

Early 20th century whalers with the body of a blue whale.

whales between 1900 and 1966. They killed 29,649 in 1931 alone. Blue whales almost became **extinct**.

In 1966, laws were passed to protect blue whales. But whalers in some countries still hunt them for oil and meat. Many blue whales are injured or die from being hit by large

The blue whale was too large for early whalers to hunt.

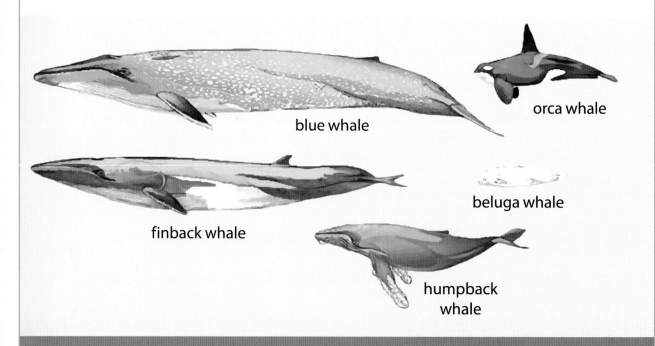

blue whale

orca whale

finback whale

beluga whale

humpback whale

BIG WHALE, TINY WAIST

Whale oil was not the only reason whales were hunted. In the 17th century, people used whale bones to make corsets. Corsets are clothing tied around women's waists. They make women's waists look smaller. Some corsets contained 60 to 100 whale bones.

ships. Some become tangled in fishing nets. Many whales show scars and injuries from these events.

Pollution and **climate change** can harm blue whales, too. Large ships pollute blue whales' ocean **habitat**. The ships release oil and chemicals into the ocean. Garbage and other waste are dumped, too. The oil and other chemicals reduce the number of krill. Blue whales have a harder time finding enough food to eat.

Large ships, such as this cargo ship, can harm blue whales.

CHAPTER THREE

HELP FOR BLUE WHALES

**Scientists are able to get close to blue whales
to learn more about them.**

Humans are to blame for the low number of blue whales. But today many people work to help the whales. Governments and international groups protect them. And scientists work to understand the whales better.

In the 1940s people began to see that blue whales were in trouble. The International Whaling Commission was formed in 1946. It began to protect whales in 1966. Today, 89 nations are members. The group makes laws about whaling throughout the world.

Blue whales are listed as endangered. They are on the International Union for Conservation and Nature and Natural Resources Red List of **threatened** animals. The Endangered Species Act also protects blue whales in U.S. waters.

The National Oceanic and Atmospheric Administration (NOAA) is a U.S. government research group. It has also come to the rescue of blue whales. The group has come up with a plan to help blue whale numbers recover. The group's scientists conduct surveys to estimate the number

SPEED LIMITS

Ships are a major threat to blue whales. Some experts think lowering ship speeds could reduce that threat. Some groups are trying to make laws that create speed limits for ships on the oceans.

of blue whales in the northern oceans. They study blue whale behavior, feeding, and movements. The group is finding ways to reduce injuries from ships. They also study the impact of pollution on blue whales. The group supports the ban on whale hunting. They also encourage efforts to prevent illegal whale hunting.

The World Wildlife Federation also studies blue whales. They use special tags to study their movements.

NOAA scientists photographed this blue whale in the Pacific Ocean.

Ocean pollution continues to harm blue whales.

They collect data to suggest protected areas for blue whales. There are many protected ocean areas around the world. Canada has nearly 800. The United States has nearly 1,800. Still, less than 3 percent of the world's

Alaska's Glacier Bay National Park and Preserve is a protected area that is home to blue whales.

oceans are protected. Perhaps in the future more countries will form protected areas. Blue whales and other ocean animals may need safe places to live.

WHAT YOU CAN DO

- Volunteer for an organization that helps save blue whales.

- Collect money in your classroom to adopt a blue whale through an organization.

- Learn about climate change and things you can do to help reduce it.

- Tell people what you have learned about blue whales and what threatens them.

GLOSSARY

climate change (KLYE-mit CHANJ) Climate change refers to significant, long-term changes in Earth's temperature, wind patterns, and rain and snowfall totals. Climate change affects blue whales' habitat.

diatoms (DI-uh-tomz) Diatoms are single-celled ocean algae. Diatoms stick to the bellies of blue whales.

endangered (en-DANE-jurd) An endangered animal is in danger of dying out. Blue whales are endangered.

equator (ee-KWAYT-ur) The equator is the imaginary line around Earth equally distant between the North and South Poles. Some blue whales migrate to the equator.

extinct (ek-STINKT) If a type of animal is extinct, all the animals have died out. Blue whales are at risk of becoming extinct.

habitat (HAB-uh-tat) A habitat is a place in nature where animals or plants live. The North Pacific Ocean is blue whale habitat.

harpoon (har-POON) A harpoon is a long spear used to hunt whales and large fish. The harpoon cannon made it possible to hunt blue whales.

krill (KRILL) Krill are small creatures that look like shrimp. Blue whales eat tons of krill every day.

mammals (MAM-alz) Mammals are animals that are warm-blooded, give birth to live young, and are usually covered with hair. Blue whales are mammals.

nostril (NOS-trul) A nostril is an opening in the nose used for breathing. The whale's blowhole is like a giant nostril.

predators (PRED-a-terz) Predators hunt, kill, and eat other animals. Blue whales have few natural predators.

threatened (THRET-und) A species that is threatened is likely to become endangered. Blue whales are listed as threatened on the International Union for Conservation and Nature and Natural Resources Red List.

whalers (WAY-lurz) Whalers are people who hunt whales. Whalers killed hundreds of thousands of blue whales before the 1960s.

TO LEARN MORE

BOOKS

Bjorklund, Ruth. *Blue Whales*. New York: Children's Press, 2014.

Marsh, Laura. *Great Migrations: Whales*. Washington, DC: National Geographic, 2010.

Smith, Molly. *Blue Whale: The World's Biggest Mammal*. New York: Bearport, 2007.

WEB SITES

Visit our Web site for links about blue whales:
childsworld.com/links

Note to Parents, Teachers, and Librarians: We routinely verify our Web links to make sure they are safe and active sites. So encourage your readers to check them out!

INDEX